In memory of Eve Merriam, 1916–1992

Photographs:
pages 2-3, 10-11, 12-13, 14-15, 16-17, 22, 23, 24-25, 27,
28-29, 30-31, and 38-39: Richie/Yamauchi Photography;
pages 4-5, 6-7, 8-9, 18-19, 20-21, 26, 32-33, 34-35, and
36-37: Ivan Chermayeff

THE HO

SIMON & SCHUSTER BOOKS FOR YOUNG READERS
An imprint of Simon & Schuster Children's Publishing
Division, 1230 Avenue of the Americas, New York,
New York 10020. Text copyright © 1995 by the Estate
of Eve Merriam. Illustrations copyright © 1995 by
Ivan Chermayeff. All rights reserved including the right
of reproduction in whole or in part in any form.
SIMON & SCHUSTER BOOKS FOR YOUNG READERS
is a trademark of Simon & Schuster. Book design by
Ivan Chermayeff. The text for this book is set in 50-point
Gill Sans. The illustrations were done in photography
and collage. Manufactured in Singapore.
10 9 8 7 6 5 4 3 2 1

Library of Congress Cataloging-in-Publication Data
Merriam, Eve, 1916-1992.   The hole story / by Eve Merriam ;
designed and illustrated by Ivan Chermayeff. p. cm.
Summary: Describes all kinds of different holes, from
straws to locks to noodles. [1. Holes—Fiction. 2. Stories
in rhyme.] I. Chermayeff, Ivan, ill. II. Title. PZ8.3.M55187Ho
1995 [E]—dc20 94-6837 CIP AC
ISBN: 0-671-88353-4

EVE MERRIAM
DESIGNED AND ILLUSTRATED BY
IVAN CHERMAYEFF

LE STORY

SIMON & SCHUSTER BOOKS FOR YOUNG READERS

HOLES

HOLES

ALL KINDS OF

HOLES

HOLES FOR SEEDS

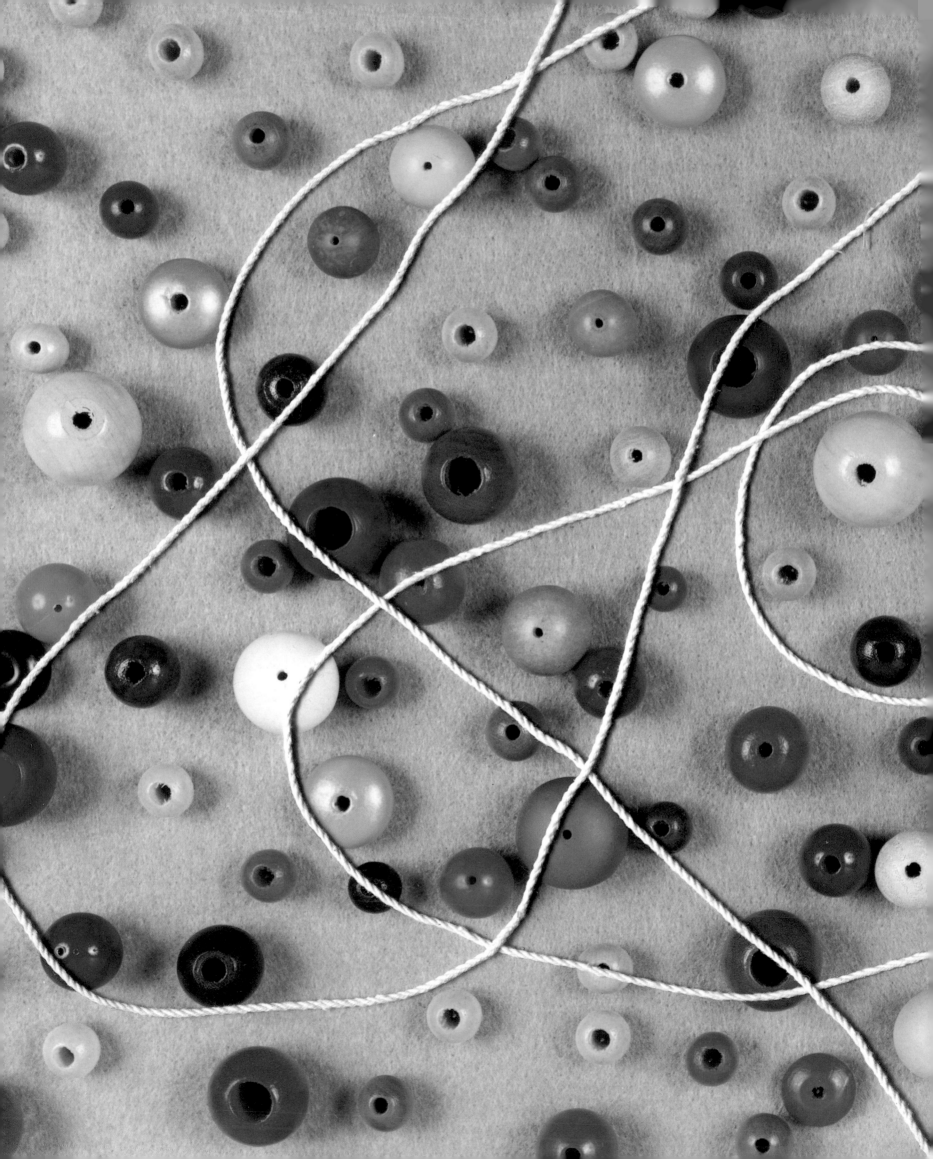

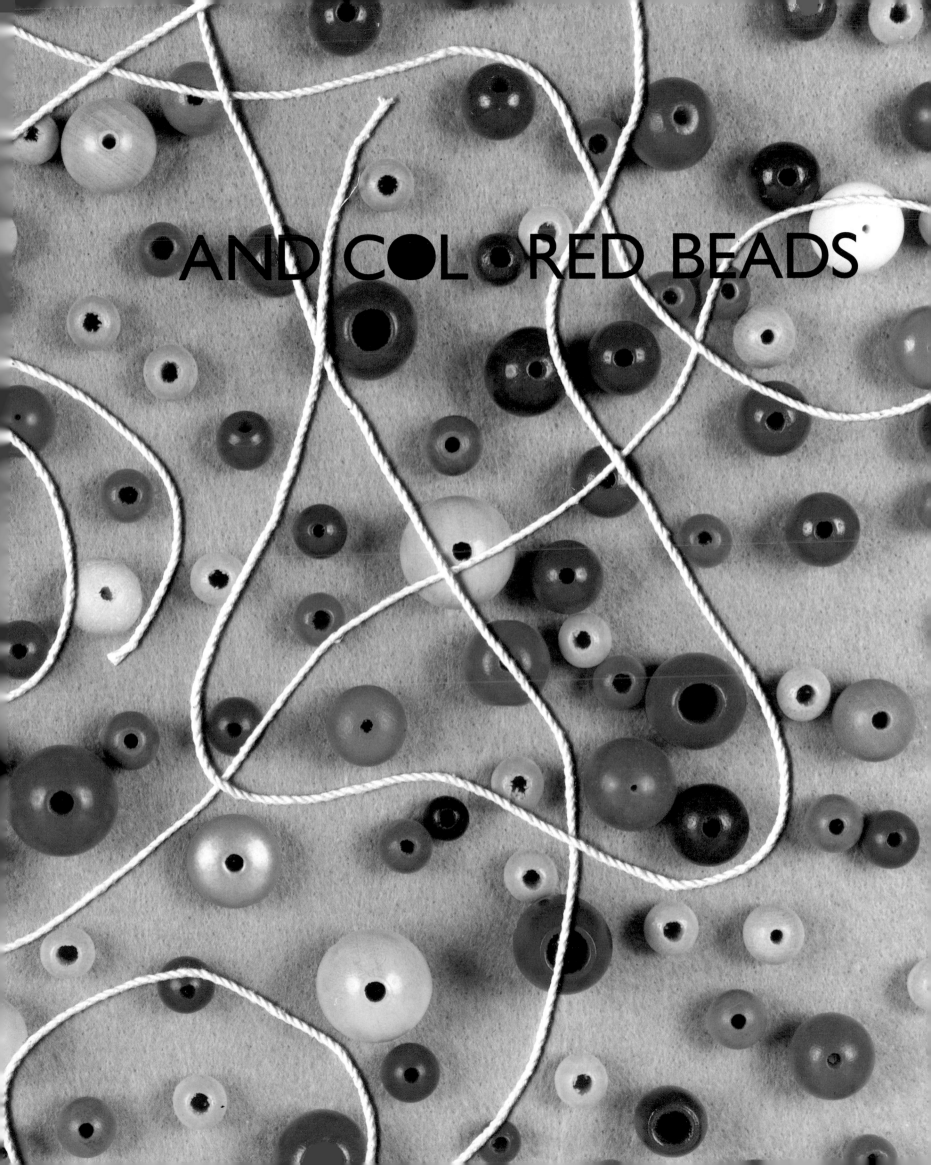

AND COLORED BEADS

HOLES TO MATCH UP

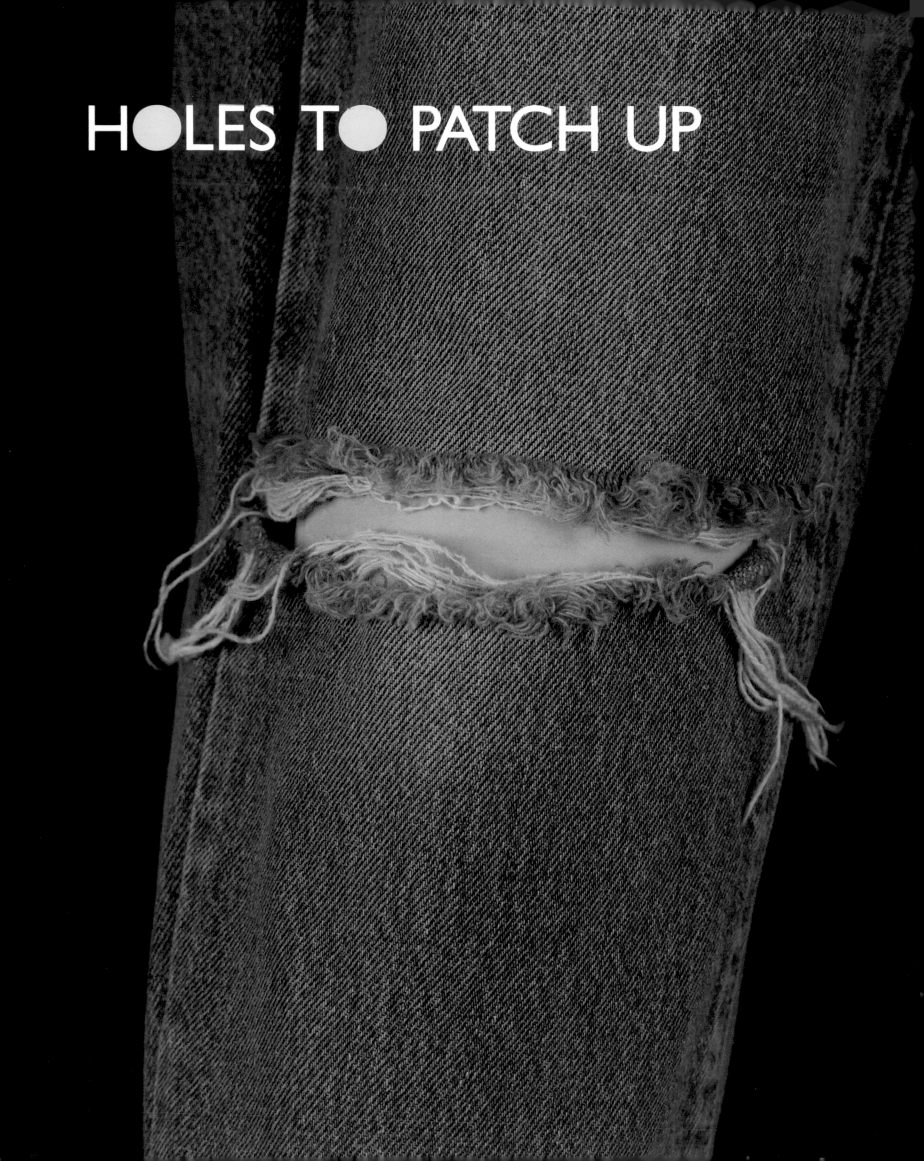

HOLES TO PATCH UP

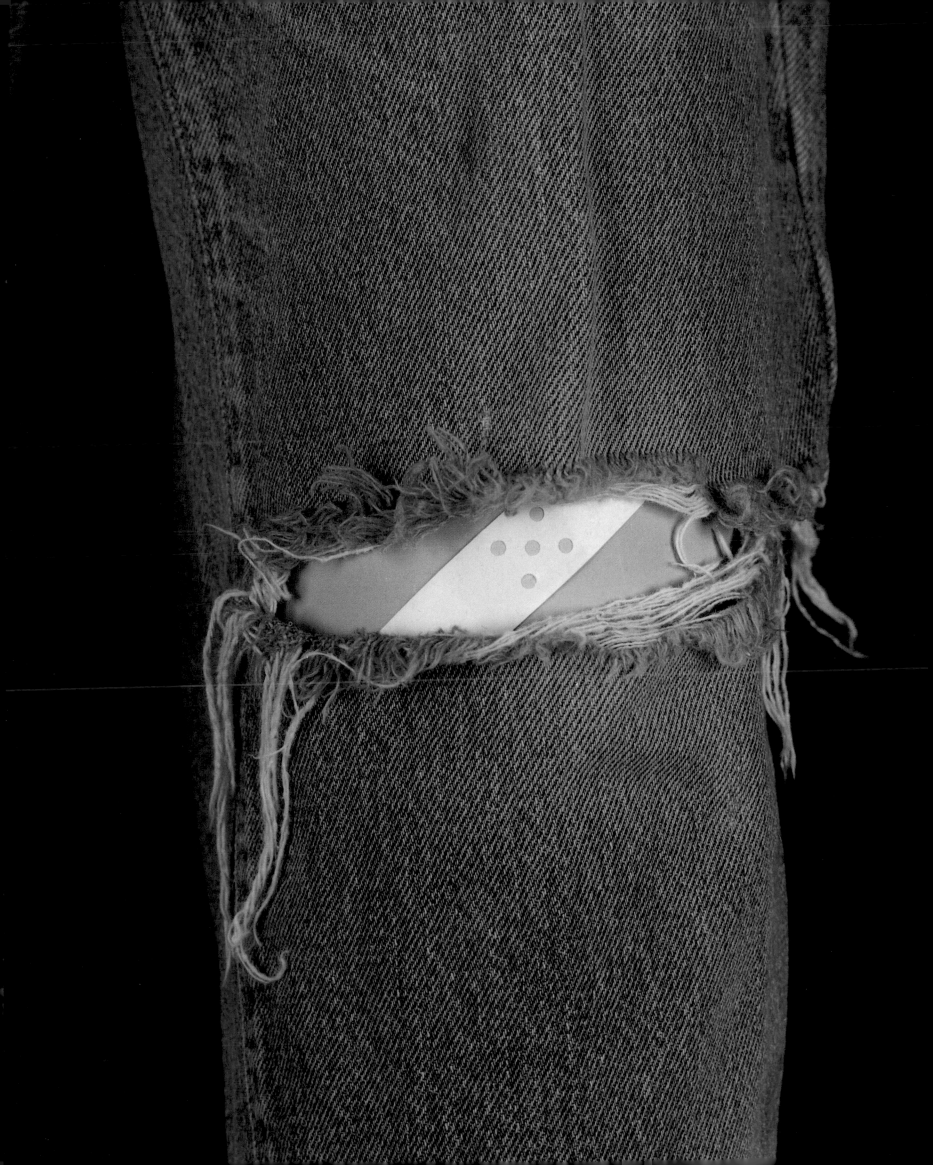

H●LES

FOR

DRINKING

TO KEEP FROM SINKING

PORTHOLES

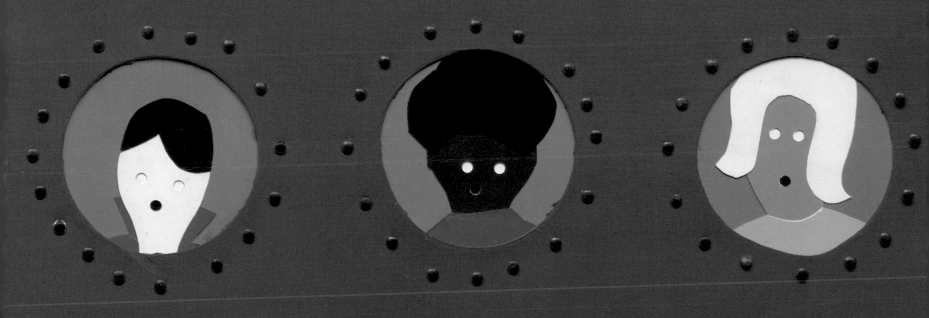

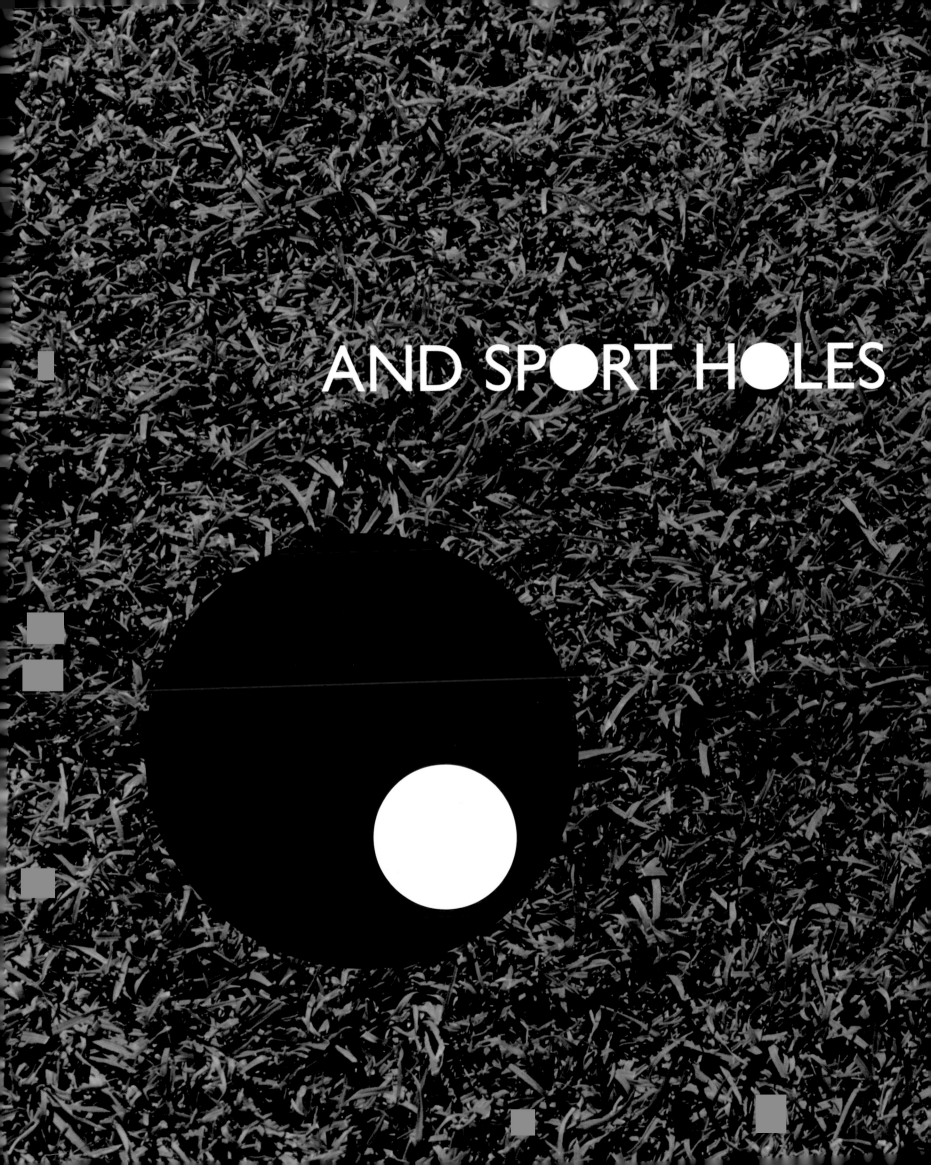

AND SPORT HOLES

A HOLE IN A SPOUT

HOLES FOR KEYS

AND HOLES FOR CHEESE

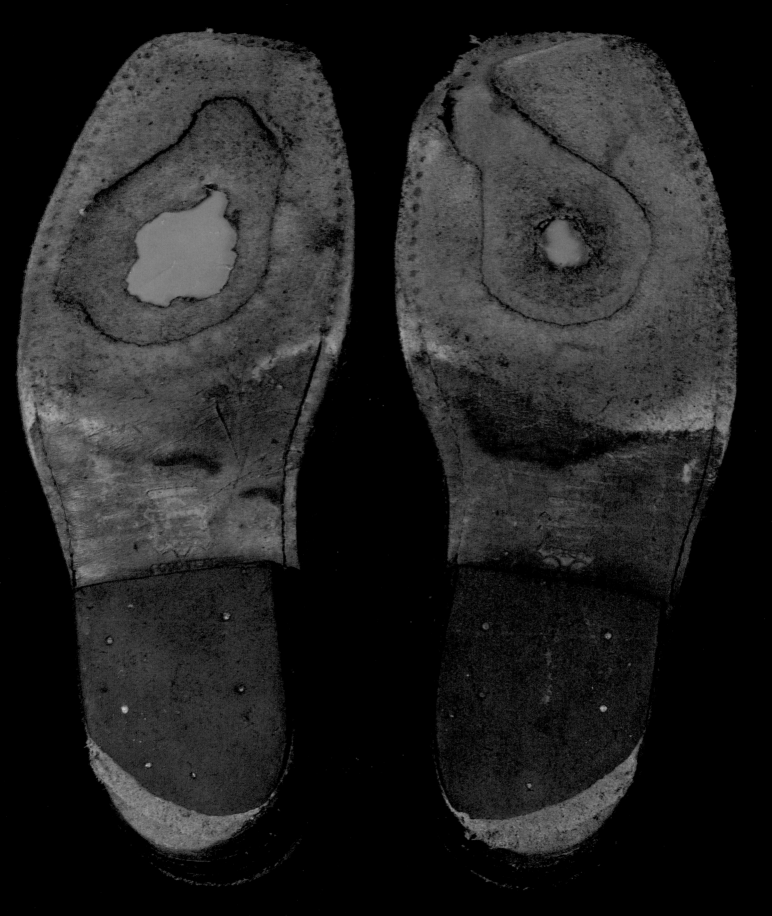

H●LES IN SANDALS

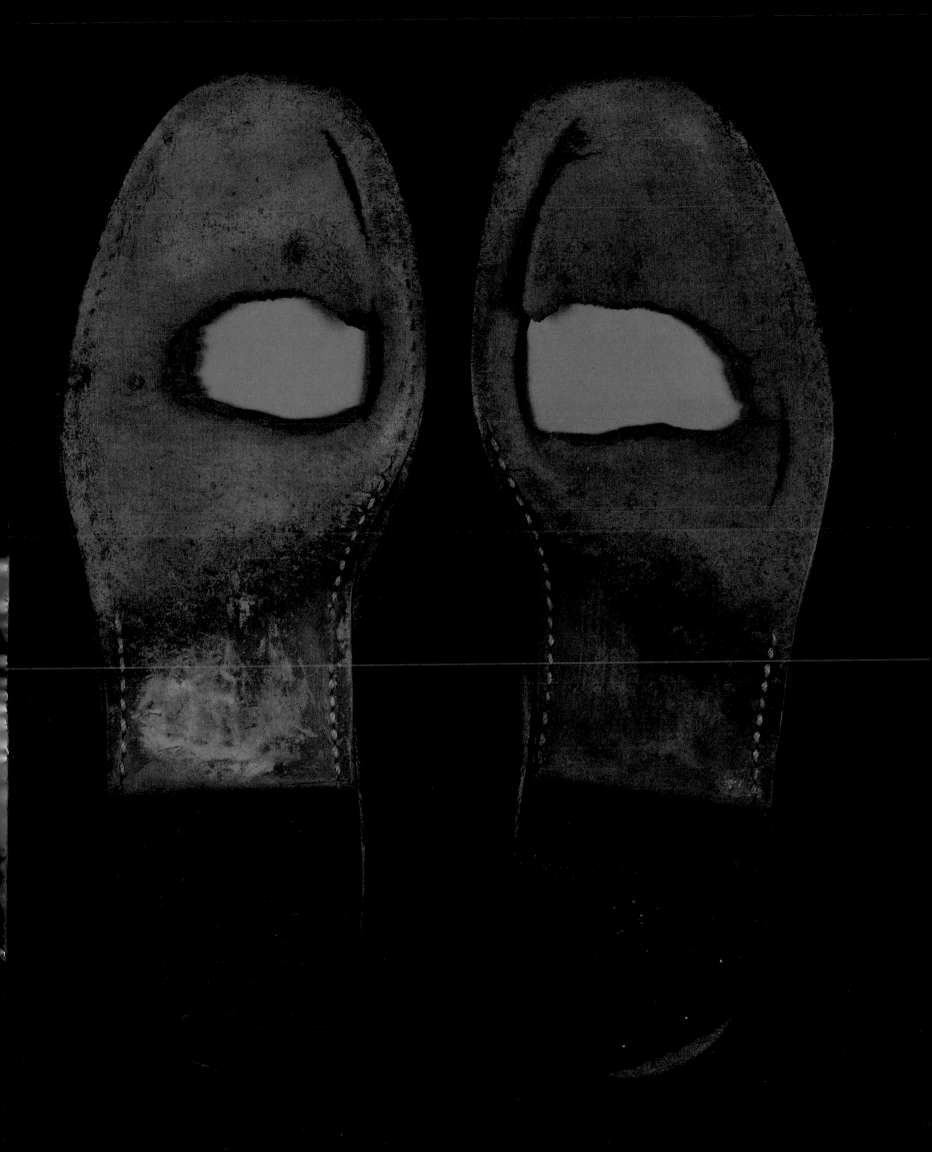

HOLES

F R

CANDLES

A HOLE FOR A WINDOW

IS THAT
THE HOLE STORY
OR
IS THERE MORE?